discover more
Marine Wildlife

Sea Mammals

Kaitlyn Salvatore

Published in 2025 by Britannica Educational Publishing (a trademark of Encyclopædia Britannica, Inc.) in association with The Rosen Publishing Group, Inc.
2544 Clinton Street, Buffalo, NY 14224

Copyright © 2025 by Encyclopædia Britannica, Inc. Britannica, Encyclopædia Britannica, and the Thistle logo are registered trademarks Encyclopædia Britannica, Inc. All rights reserved.

Rosen Publishing materials copyright © 2025 The Rosen Publishing Group, Inc. All rights reserved.

Distributed exclusively by Rosen Publishing.
To see additional Britannica Educational Publishing titles, go to rosenpublishing.com.

All rights reserved. No part of this book may be reproduced in any form without permission in writing from the publisher, except by a reviewer.

Editor: Brianna Propis
Book Design: Michael Flynn

Photo Credits: Cover Longjourneys/Shutterstock.com; (series background) Dai Yim/Shutterstock.com; p. 4 Gema Alvarez Fernandez/Shutterstock.com; p. 5 Thierry Eidenweil/Shutterstock.com; p. 6 Danita Delimont/Shutterstock.com; p. 7 Vladimir Melnik/Shutterstock.com; p. 9 (top) Zaruba Ondrej/Shutterstock.com; p. 9 (bottom) Martin Prochazkacz/Shutterstock.com; p. 11 (top) Belovodchenko Anton/Shutterstock.com; p. 11 (bottom) Imagine Earth Photography/Shutterstock.com; p. 12 Vladimir Turkenich/Shutterstock.com; p. 13 A7880S/Shutterstock.com; p. 15 (top) FOTO JOURNEY/Shutterstock.com; p. 15 (bottom) LouieLea/Shutterstock.com; p. 16 aleksandard/Shutterstock.com; p. 17 Wirestock Creators/Shutterstock.com; p. 18 Zaruba Ondrej/Shutterstock.com; p. 19 Robert Harding Video/Shutterstock.com; p. 20 vkilikov/Shutterstock.com; p. 21 Animanish/Shutterstock.com; p. 22 seo byeong gon/Shutterstock.com; p. 23 Christopher Teixeira/Shutterstock.com; p. 25 Marcelorpc/Shutterstock.com; p. 25 Wildnerdpix/Shutterstock.com; p. 26 Sven Hansche/Shutterstock.com; p. 27 Mr.anaked/Shutterstock.com; p. 28 Vladimir Turkenich/Shutterstock.com; p. 29 AlexFilim/Shutterstock.com.

Library of Congress Cataloging-in-Publication Data

Names: Salvatore, Kaitlyn, author.
Title: Sea mammals / Kaitlyn Salvatore.
Description: [Buffalo] : Britannica Educational Publishing, [2025] | Series: Discover more : marine wildlife | Includes bibliographical references and index.
Identifiers: LCCN 2024029557 | ISBN 9781641903639 (library binding) | ISBN 9781641903622 (paperback) | ISBN 9781641903646 (ebook)
Subjects: LCSH: Marine mammals--Juvenile literature.
Classification: LCC QL713.2 .S25 2025 | DDC 599.5--dc23/eng/20240726
LC record available at https://lccn.loc.gov/2024029557

Manufactured in the United States of America

Some of the images in this book illustrate individuals who are models. The depictions do not imply actual situations or events.

CPSIA Compliance Information: Batch #CWBRIT25. For further information contact Rosen Publishing at 1-800-237-9932.

Contents

Underwater Home.........................4

What Are Mammals?....................6

Mammal Babies......................10

Whales............................12

Mammals with Flippers...............16

Sea Cows..........................20

Ice Bears.........................22

Old Men of the Sea 24

Marine Mammals in Danger 26

Glossary........................30

For More Information................31

Index...........................32

Underwater Home

A fish spends its whole life underwater without ever needing to come up for air, but whales must rise to the surface to breathe. This is because whales—unlike fish—are mammals.

Mammals are animals that breathe air, have backbones, and grow hair. All female mammals produce milk for their babies. Animals that are considered mammals are some of the smartest living creatures on Earth. Humans are mammals too.

Humpback whales have hair on their head, mouth, and flippers. The golf-ball-sized lumps on their head contain a hair follicle, or an opening on the skin where hair grows.

Manatees live their whole lives in the water. They're great swimmers that can swim upside down or do somersaults.

Marine mammals are mammals that live in the world's oceans. Some marine mammals include whales, seals, sea lions, walruses, manatees, polar bears, and sea otters. Certain marine mammals—such as whales—live their whole lives in the water. Others, such as polar bears, spend part of their lives on land.

Consider This

Sharks also live in the ocean, but they're fish. What differences does a shark's body have compared to a whale's body?

What Are Mammals?

Mammals are the only animals able to produce milk to feed their babies. Females have special **glands** called mammary glands. After childbirth, the mother's glands produce milk. The mother feeds the young with this milk until the young are old enough to get food for themselves. Marine mammal milk has a lot of fat in it. This helps the babies grow quickly.

To keep warm, sea otters spend a large portion of their days grooming and conditioning their fur.

This mother harp seal is nursing her pup.

All mammals have hair at some stage of development. Some marine mammals have more than others. For example, the thick fur coat of sea otters keeps them warm in the cold waters where they live. On the other hand, whales have very little hair. Some whales have hair only before they are born. Blubber keeps them warm instead. Some marine mammals, such as fur seals, have both thick coats of fur and blubber.

WORD WISE
GLANDS ARE ORGANS THAT MAKE SUBSTANCES SUCH AS SWEAT, MILK, AND TEARS.

Mammals are warm-blooded, meaning they can keep their body at roughly the same temperature no matter what the surrounding temperature is. This allows marine mammals to live in waters with a wide range of temperatures.

All mammals breathe air. They use the oxygen in the air to make the energy their body needs. The body of a marine mammal can store extra oxygen. This lets them hold their breath for a long time underwater. They still need to visit the surface to breathe, though.

Mammals have highly developed brains. Their complex brain allows mammals to learn from experience and adapt their behavior. Marine biologists, or scientists who study marine animals, have found that whales are among the most intelligent mammals.

Some marine animals, like polar bears, prefer to live alone. Others, like walruses, prefer to live in groups.

compare and contrast

Why might living in a group be helpful to an animal? How could it be difficult? Think about predators and food sources.

Sperm whales have the largest brain of any animal on the planet.

Mammal Babies

To reproduce, a male mammal mates with a female mammal. Females carry the developing young in their body after mating. The young develop inside a part of their mother's body called the uterus. They receive nutrition through their mother's body.

Gestation, or the length of time that the mother carries the young in the uterus, varies between species. Most whales are pregnant from 9 to 12 months. Marine mammals give birth to live young. Most marine mammals give birth to just one baby at a time.

Whale, dolphin, manatee, and dugong babies are called calves. Baby seals, sea lions, walruses, and sea otters are pups, while baby polar bears are cubs. These babies, along with other kinds of baby mammals, learn behaviors from their parents.

All marine mammals except polar bears have only one baby at a time. Some marine mammals, like walruses, have one baby every two to three years.

compare and contrast

Fish can have thousands of babies at a time, while mammals typically have much fewer. How might fish parents be different from mammal parents? How could they be similar?

Whale calves are born knowing how to swim. They learn how to jump in and out of water from watching their mother.

Whales

Cetacea is the name for the group of animals that whales belong to. This group also includes dolphins and porpoises. People often confuse dolphins and porpoises, although dolphins are usually larger and have longer, beaklike snouts.

Whales live in oceans around the world. Large species often **migrate** long distances. The shape of a whale's body helps it move quickly through the water. It pushes its tail up and down to move. The tail is divided into two broad sections called flukes. Whales steer with their flippers.

Orcas, also known as killer whales, aren't even whales—they're dolphins!

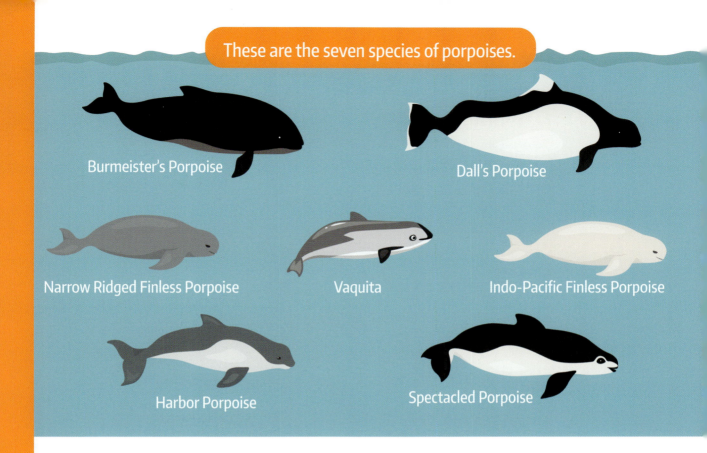

There are two basic kinds of whales: toothed and baleen. Toothed whales have sharp teeth and eat mainly fish and squid. There are about 70 species of toothed whales. These include sperm whales, belugas, narwhals, beaked whales, and pilot whales. Dolphins and porpoises are also members of this group.

WORD WISE
MIGRATION IS WHEN ANIMALS MOVE FROM ONE PLACE TO ANOTHER TO FIND FOOD OR REPRODUCE.

There are 10 different species of baleen whales. These include blue whales, gray whales, fin whales, humpback whales, sei whales, and right whales. Instead of teeth, these whales have blade-shaped plates called baleen hanging from the roof of their mouth. The inner sides of the baleen have bristles that trap food. A baleen whale feeds by swimming with its mouth open or by gulping water. The baleen acts as a filter, letting out water but holding in small fish, shrimp, and other creatures.

Whales make many sounds, including whistles, barks, and screams, to communicate with other whales. Toothed whales make special sounds to locate objects they cannot see. These sounds bounce off solid surfaces and travel back to the whale's sensitive ears in a process called echolocation.

The shape of a whale's baleen helps them eat their prey. Short baleen plates help whales eat fish, while long baleen plates help them hunt smaller animals like zooplankton.

compare and contrast

Whales breathe through an opening on top of their head called a blowhole. Humans breathe air through their nostrils and mouths. Compare and contrast the two ways both mammals breathe.

Toothed whales use echolocation to hunt prey. They send out clicking sounds to see if echoes come back from their prey!

Mammals with Flippers

There are two groups of seals: earless seals and eared seals. Earless seals do have ears, but they do not stick out. Eared seals have **visible** ears. Sea lions are eared seals that sometimes have thick fur around their neck that looks like a lion's mane. Fur seals are several species of eared seal that are known for their thick coats.

Seals are related to walruses. A walrus looks like a big seal with two large upper teeth called tusks. These tusks stick down from the walrus's mouth.

> Seals can sleep in water in a position called bottling. This is when their body—except for their snout—remains completely underwater.

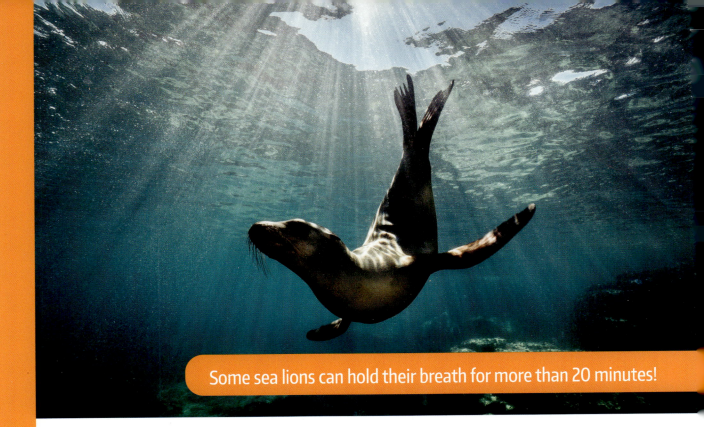

Some sea lions can hold their breath for more than 20 minutes!

Instead of legs, seals and walruses have two pairs of flippers. The flippers help them swim. Eared seals and walruses can turn their rear flippers forward under their body. This allows them to scoot around while on land. Earless seals cannot turn their rear flippers forward. To move on land, they wriggle on their belly or push themselves forward using their front flippers.

WORD WISE
VISIBLE MEANS ABLE TO BE SEEN.

Seals are found throughout the world. They are especially common in seas near the North and South Poles. Some species like the open ocean. Others prefer to live along the coast. All seals spend some time on islands, beaches, or sheets of ice. They come ashore to breed.

Seals eat mostly fish. Some also eat squid and shellfish. The leopard seal of the Antarctic feeds on penguins and other seals.

Walruses cuddle their babies the same way humans do!

In the wild, gray seals can live up to 35 years.

Walruses live in the cold Arctic seas of Europe, Asia, and North America. Walruses eat many things, especially clams. They dig clams from the seafloor with their tusks. They shovel food into their mouth with their whiskers. Walruses live in groups that can include more than 100 animals. Most of their time is spent in the ocean, but they rest on ice or rocky islands at times.

Consider This

Male seals often fight other male seals for the right to mate with a female. How do you think they fight?

Sea Cows

Manatees—also known as sea cows—and dugongs look very similar. This is because they are closely related. However, there are some differences. Manatees have a flat, rounded tail. The dugong has a deeply notched tail, or fluke, as do whales and dolphins.

Both animals live in warm coastal waters. However, the dugong lives in the Indian and Pacific Oceans, while most manatees live in the Atlantic Ocean. Some manatees also live in South America's Amazon River.

Much like dolphins, dugongs use chirps, whistles, barks, and other sounds that echo underwater to communicate with each other.

The average adult manatee is about 10 feet long (3 m) and weighs between 800 and 1,200 pounds (363 to 544 kg).

Manatees and dugongs are slow-moving, peaceful animals. Unlike most other marine mammals, they are herbivores, or plant eaters. They use their flippers to push food toward their mouth.

Manatees live alone or in small family groups. Dugongs are most often seen alone or in pairs. Although herds of 200 dugongs have been seen, it is very rare.

Consider This

Manatees don't have any natural predators. However, humans are a threat to manatees through boating accidents and destruction of their underwater habitats. How might humans be viewed as their predator in this case?

Ice Bears

Polar bears (sometimes called ice bears) live in Earth's Arctic regions. They spend a lot of their time on sea ice. They can travel long distances on the ice floes that drift through Arctic waters.

Polar bears mostly live alone. They feed mainly on other sea mammals, especially seals. They are good hunters, but they also will eat dead fish, stranded whales, and even garbage. Polar bears hunt both on the ice and in the water. They are good but unusual swimmers: they use only their front legs to swim.

Polar bears can swim for long distances at speeds up to 6 miles (9.7 km) per hour to get from one piece of ice to another.

Under its white (actually transparent, or clear) fur, a polar bear's skin is black.

In winter, a female polar bear gives birth in a snowy den. She has one to four tiny cubs at a time. She nurses them for about two years. Afterward, the cubs stay with their mother for a few more years until they are **mature** enough to mate.

WORD WISE
MATURE IS A WORD FOR A LIVING THING THAT IS FULLY GROWN AND PHYSICALLY DEVELOPED.

Old Men of the Sea

A sea otter's body is built for the ocean. Its webbed feet are good for swimming. Unlike many animals, sea otters can safely drink salt water. This allows them to remain at sea for several days at a time.

Sea otters are nicknamed the "old men of the sea." This is because their fur turns from brown to white as they get older and because of their whiskers.

Sea otters help control the sea urchin population. When there are fewer sea urchins, kelp forests are healthier.

Sea otters live along the Pacific coast of North America. They are usually **solitary** but are sometimes seen in groups. Gatherings of up to 2,000 have been seen along the coast of Alaska. At night, sea otters may choose to sleep on land or simply to float near beds of seaweed. Sea otters eat sea urchins, crabs, shellfish, and fish. They usually eat while floating on their back. They often use rocks to break open crabs and shellfish. They crush sea urchins with their forefeet and teeth. Female sea otters give birth to one pup at a time in the water. The pup remains under the care of its mother for six to eight months.

WORD WISE
SOLITARY ANIMALS PREFER TO SPEND MOST OF THEIR TIME ALONE.

Marine Mammals in Danger

Humans have hunted marine mammals for thousands of years. These animals are hunted for their meat, hides, blubber, and fur. Many species of large whales became endangered, or at risk of dying out completely, as a result. Sea otters and seal species became endangered as well because they were hunted for their fur. It wasn't until the 20th century that countries began passing laws to protect marine mammals and help them increase in number.

Whales and dolphins rely on echolocation to navigate through the ocean and find food. Loud noises from ships, drilling rigs, and other human sources disrupt their ability to communicate.

Marine mammals might mistake water **pollution** such as plastic for food. This can cause serious health problems for the animals.

Still, people continue to do harmful things to marine mammals. Dolphins become tangled in and killed by fishing nets. Pollution harms these animals too. It can make marine mammals sick and kill off the animals and plants they depend on for food. Oil spills hurt all marine mammals, but sea otters are especially harmed. When oil coats their fur, sea otters cannot keep warm.

WORD WISE
POLLUTION IS ANYTHING THAT MAKES EARTH DIRTY OR UNHEALTHY. THIS INCLUDES WASTE OR CHEMICALS.

Global warming is the slow increase of Earth's average temperature, which causes many problems for marine mammals. When people burn oil, gas, and coal to power factories, drive cars, and generate electricity, certain gases are released into Earth's atmosphere. These gases trap the sun's heat and keep Earth warm. Too much of the sun's heat is trapped when a large amount of these gases is released into the atmosphere.

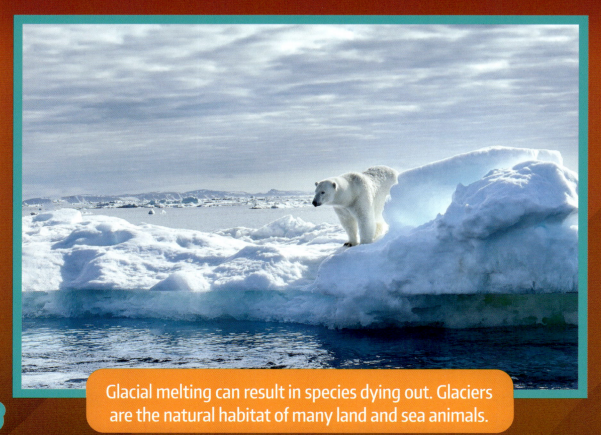

Glacial melting can result in species dying out. Glaciers are the natural habitat of many land and sea animals.

Millions of vehicles drop small amounts of oil each day onto roads and parking lots. Much of it eventually makes its way to the sea.

Global warming is causing the ice in the Arctic to melt. This means polar bears have less space in which to hunt and mate. Melting ice also causes the sea levels to rise. Life in the ocean is threatened by increased sea levels and warmer water temperatures. These things cause underwater ecosystems to become unbalanced. People need to work together to reduce fossil fuel emissions and help protect marine wildlife.

Consider This

One way people help reduce fossil fuel emissions is by using solar power, or energy from the sun, to produce electricity. What are other ways to help reduce the release of gases into the atmosphere?

Glossary

atmosphere The whole mass of air surrounding Earth.

blubber The fat of whales and other large sea mammals.

echolocation A process for locating distant or invisible objects by means of sound waves reflected back to the sender from the objects.

flipper A broad flat limb (of a seal or whale) used for swimming.

fluke One of the two parts of a whale's or dugong's tail.

fossil fuel A natural fuel formed inside of Earth, such as coal and natural gas.

marine In or from the sea.

nostril An outer opening of the nose for breathing.

organ A body part that consists of cells and tissues and is specialized to do a particular task.

oxygen A gas that is found in the air and is necessary for the survival of all plants and animals.

sea urchin Round sea animals with spines that live on the sea floor.

species A class of living things of the same kind and with the same name.

temperature A measure of how hot or cold something is.

webbed Having fingers or toes that are joined by a membrane, or a thin layer of skin.

For More Information

Books

Gibbons, Gail. *Whales*. New York, NY: Holiday House, 2022.

Jaycox, Jaclyn. *Sea Otters*. North Mankato, MN: Pebble, 2022.

Koran, Maria. *Marine Mammals*. New York, NY: AV² by Weigl, 2020.

Websites

Curious Kids–Whale and Dolphin Conservation
uk.whales.org/kidzone/curious-kids
Learn more interesting facts about whales and dolphins.

Fun Water Mammal Facts for Kids
easyscienceforkids.com/all-about-water-mammals/
Read more fun facts about marine mammals and look at cool pictures of them.

Marine Mammals
www.youtube.com/watch?v=4JcZGRqUJvs
Watch your favorite marine mammals in action and review the individual species.

Publisher's note to educators and parents: Our editors have carefully reviewed these websites to ensure that they are suitable for students. Many websites change frequently, however, and we cannot guarantee that a site's future contents will continue to meet our high standards of quality and educational value. Be advised that students should be closely supervised whenever they access the internet.

Index

B

baleen whales, 13, 14, 15
blowhole, 15
brain, 8

D

dolphins, 10, 12, 13, 20, 26, 27
dugongs, 10, 20, 21

E

ecolocation, 14, 15, 26

F

fat/blubber, 6, 7, 26
flippers, 4, 12, 16, 17, 21
flukes, 12, 20
fur, 6, 7, 16, 23, 24, 26, 27

H

hair, 4, 7

I

ice, 18, 19, 22, 29

M

manatees, 5, 10, 20, 21
milk, 4, 6, 7

P

polar bears, 5, 9, 10, 11, 22, 23, 29
porpoises, 12, 13

S

sea lions, 5, 10, 16, 17
seals, 5, 7, 10, 16, 17, 18, 19, 22, 26
sea otters, 5, 6, 7, 10, 24, 25, 26, 27

T

tail, 12, 20
teeth, 13, 14, 16, 25
temperature, 8, 28, 29
toothed whales, 13, 14, 15
tusks, 16, 19

W

walruses, 5, 9, 11, 16, 17, 18, 19
whales, 4, 5, 7, 8, 9, 10, 11, 12, 13, 14, 15,
    20, 22, 26